YOUR KNOWLEDGE HAS VALUE

- We will publish your bachelor's and
  master's thesis, essays and papers

- Your own eBook and book -
  sold worldwide in all relevant shops

- Earn money with each sale

Upload your text at www.GRIN.com
and publish for free

Hemant Kumar Saini

Backdoor Add-ons. A new way to harbor the data

GRIN Publishing

Bibliographic information published by the German National Library:

The German National Library lists this publication in the National Bibliography; detailed bibliographic data are available on the Internet at http://dnb.dnb.de .

Imprint:

Copyright © 2014 GRIN Verlag GmbH
Print and binding: Books on Demand GmbH, Norderstedt Germany
ISBN: 978-3-656-82924-9

This book at GRIN:

http://www.grin.com/en/e-book/283433/backdoor-add-ons-a-new-way-to-harbor-the-data

Backdoor Add-ons

A new way to harbor the data

Hemant Kumar Saini

M.Tech

Department of Computer Science & Engineerin,

RTU, Kota

Foreword

Mr. Hemant Kumar Saini is a Red hat Certified Engineer. He is pursuing M. Tech in Computer Science & Engineering from Rajasthan Technical University, Kota. He has completed his B. Tech in Information Technology from MLV Government Textile & Engineering College. He is having 2 years of industrial experience and one year of academic experience. His research interests are Computer Network and Cyber Security.

Table of Contents

1. Introduction

Today in the growing era of communication everyone wants to update with the new functionality so that they would survive with the best. Since the only way to access Internet is the browser, so it is vital to configure them securely. With the growing demands to ease the work in one click many engine tools, supportive plug-ins have been developed for web-browser. And the users also without knowing its causes quickly installed such extensible plug-ins in their browsers which gives the chances to intruders to get control their computer without their knowledge. Such plug-ins becomes victim for the vulnerabilities of the computer which are due to the manufacturer coding fault.

2. Deep Understanding the malicious Add-ons

With the programming perspective, Browser extensions are the small set of instructions which performs the specific task for enhancing the functionality of the web browsers. But as we stick to specific computing then these extensions are the small application that has to be installed on the browser which changes the skin, adding the special features like flash player, java virtual machine and some customizations for the password or Email enhancements and so named as *Add-ons*. Since all such add-ons are the legitimate and helpful in tailoring the professional utilities but somehow in the market many malfunctioners develop the add-ons which extract the information from the surfing and compromise the security and privacy of the user. Such applications are the root cause of malicious add-ons.

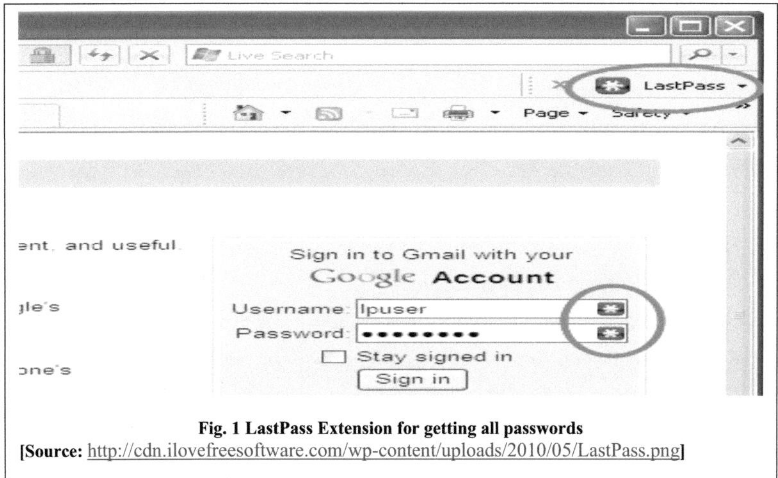

Fig. 1 LastPass Extension for getting all passwords
[**Source:** http://cdn.ilovefreesoftware.com/wp-content/uploads/2010/05/LastPass.png]

Most of the browsers allow the third party installation mechanism which acts a host for performing the malicious activity by the hackers. Different extensions are being developed for different purposes but these installations would not only add the features but also sometimes become a way to intrude into the system due to non-secure coding or non-secure configuration. As such, the Firefox default configuration to store the last work pertaining the way to give idea what the last has been accessed on the computer. With such an enhanced facility intruder find their way to get control over the autoform fillings which is stored in the browser and try their practices.

As Balazs depicted in Fig.1 about the detailed structure for the insertion of a malware into legitimate extension for Firefox. Since the browser extensions are the Application Programming Interface (API) and the LastPass is one of the Firefox extensions which support the authentication using the master password mechanism. It allows the users with strong, individual passwords for every online service by having only one master password to unlock the other information. Unfortunately, if the attacker alters the LastPass's code and somehow reveals the master password then it gets all the saved content. And this all can be practiced in less than two hours work. That's why the new browsers do not allow the third party installations, so that, if the extensions malice and the browser vendor come to know about the vulnerability into its extensions it can be improved further to overcome such threats.

3. Case Study with Chrome Extensions

Various chrome extensions have been developed for exploiting the security risks. We study some of the useful cases with their practical implementation.

Case Study1: Bang! For Email Spam

Today the most notorious cause for email spam is the botnet. As the spammer sends the spamming commands to bots, they send spam's to victims through HTTP (hyper text transfer protocol) request. This spam information has been stored in the file named *spam.txt* under the extension directory as shown in Fig.2 (a) which includes the victim's mail id. Hence it uses the same legitimate email account to send spam as when the user logins which can be seen in Fig. 2(b). Here, Bang! is chosen as a bot extension to monitor login users and the iPlanet mail system is used for experiment. Since this extension has the privilege of *"tabs"* which listens to notification of tabs with the method of *chrome.tabs.onUpdated.addListener().*With this credential information, an HTTP request to the iPlanet mail server is authorized to take any action on behalf of the user, instead of sending the username and password in each transaction. As shown in Fig.2(c) the extension sends out the HTTP requests, which in turn triggers the web serverto send spam emails to the victim. And as the victim email address can be embedded in the extension (as in *spam.txt*), the bot can always obtain new victim emails by updating the extension from the botnet master's server, which is allowed by default in the Chrome ecosystem.

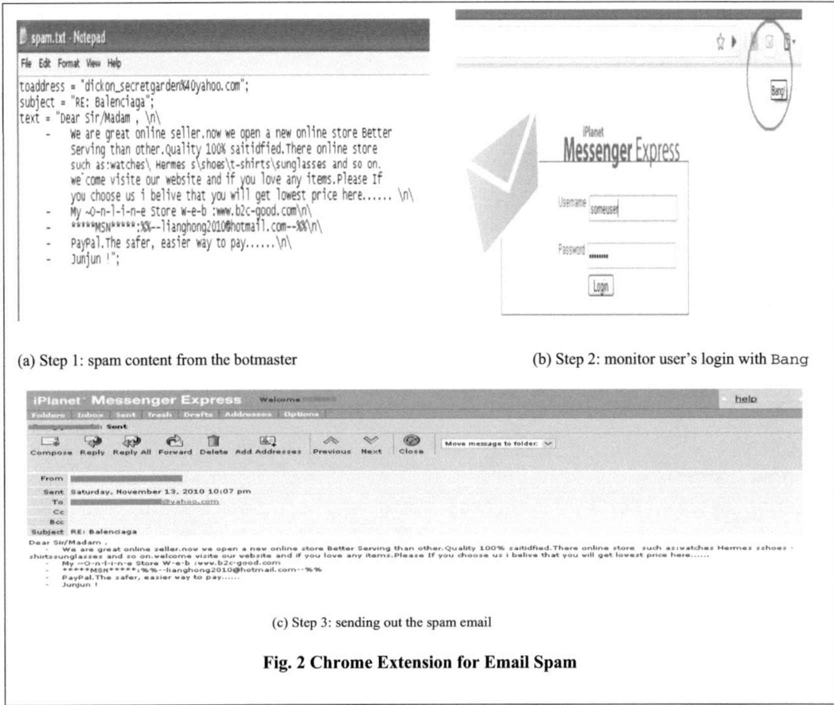

(a) Step 1: spam content from the botmaster   (b) Step 2: monitor user's login with Bang

(c) Step 3: sending out the spam email

Fig. 2 Chrome Extension for Email Spam

Case Study2: Bang for Password Sniffing

Nowadays, online shopping is becoming very popular due to which sensitive information such as bank account and password is often saved by the web browser, temporarily or permanently, which makes web browsers a major target of spyware. When the victim web page is loaded, Bang! injects content script into the web page, which can access all DOM (Document Object Model) elements including the form with the user name and password. Such information can then be sent to the designated email address. In order to access sensitive information in the Chrome browser, our extension needs to access the DOM tree of a web page. Therefore it needs the cross-site permission to insert the content script when a web page is rendered. When the user browses the page from

7

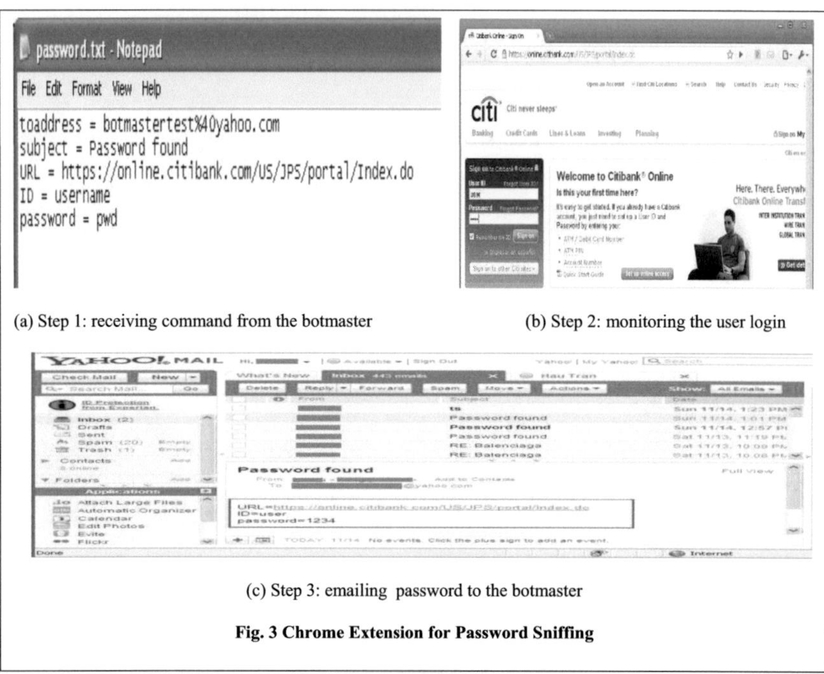

(a) Step 1: receiving command from the botmaster

(b) Step 2: monitoring the user login

(c) Step 3: emailing password to the botmaster

Fig. 3 Chrome Extension for Password Sniffing

online.citibank.com, two content scripts (*jquery.js* and *myscript.js*) are injected into the target web page, and the JavaScripts have full privileges to access all DOM elements including the form with username and password. With the received command shown in Fig. 3(a), *myscript.js* reads the values of user name and password elements when the user inputs, as shown in Fig. 3(b), and sends to a designated email address. Fig. 3(c) shows that the password information is successfully.

4. Secure over malicious Add-ons

Since the new add-ons are developing much fast in the Web market, we can't test each and every extension over the security trends and list out which one is safe for our browsers. Hence to overcome on security issues we can take some countermeasures which help us to overcome such threats.

1. Block third-party cookies: Cookies are an important component of Internet usability so instead of turning them off altogether, third-party cookies would be blocked.

2. Beware of autocomplete: The autocomplete or autofill feature saves the recently information that has been surfed, even the personal login information. So   autocomplete for login information poses a big threat if hardware somehow intruded.

3. Restrict add-on: Add-ons harbors the malware and tries to attack the browser code. Hence, browsers should be configured such that they will prompt before installing add-ons..

4. Enable content filters: Most of the browsers store a database of phishing and malware sites to block the threat contents. Users must enable such content filters.

5. Turn on popup blockers: Popups can inject malware directly by clicking on small advertisements using Web engineering tricks. This popup blocking must be enabled to protect from wrong clicks.

5. Concluding Remarks

Malware developers have increasingly exploited browser extensions for various attacks in recent years. Through the depth analysis, one can find the issues that are rooted from the coarse-grained privilege management for the extension components and undifferentiated access permissions for DOM elements in web pages.

The changes to the browser allow only extensions to be loaded, and detect unauthorized changes made to installed extensions. This modification seals the outside installation vector for malicious extensions by disallowing standard and injection type installations external to a browser session. One can enabled the browser to monitor a significant portion of extension code at runtime and effect policy on a per-extension basis. More research is needed for designing a comprehensive suite of policies that can be enforced on extensions with acceptable overheads on usability.

- SmartScreen Filter can be used to prevent from phishing attacks, frauds, and malicious websites.

- Highlighting the domain avoids phishing websites that use pseudo web addresses to trick. The true domain is always spotlight in the address bar.

- Cross site scripting (XSS) filter detect the attacks from phishing and fraudulent websites that sneaks the personal and financial information

- A 128-bit secure (SSL) connection provides the best protection for the sensitive financial transactions over the internet.

6. References

[1] Malicious browser extensions pose a serious threat and defenses are lacking, http://www.pcworld.com/article/2049540/malicious-browser-extensions-pose-a-serious-threat-and-defenses-are-lacking.html

[2] Liu, L., Zhang, X., Yan, G., & Chen, S. (2012, February). Chrome extensions: Threat analysis and countermeasures. In *Network and Distributed System Security Symposium (NDSS).*

[3] Sun software product map, http://www.oracle.com/us/sun/sun-products-map-075562.html

[4] Most spam comes from just six botnets, http://en.wikipedia.org/wiki/Usage_share_of_web_browsers

[5] Understanding security and safer computing http://windows.microsoft.com/en-IN/windows7/Understanding-security-and-safer-computing